Outreach Ministry at Its Best

ISBN-13: 978-1530174102

ISBN-10: 1530174104

Outreach Ministry is a form of serving. As the old saying goes; "we cannot lead unless we know how to serve."

Many have given their life possessions over to outreach ministry.

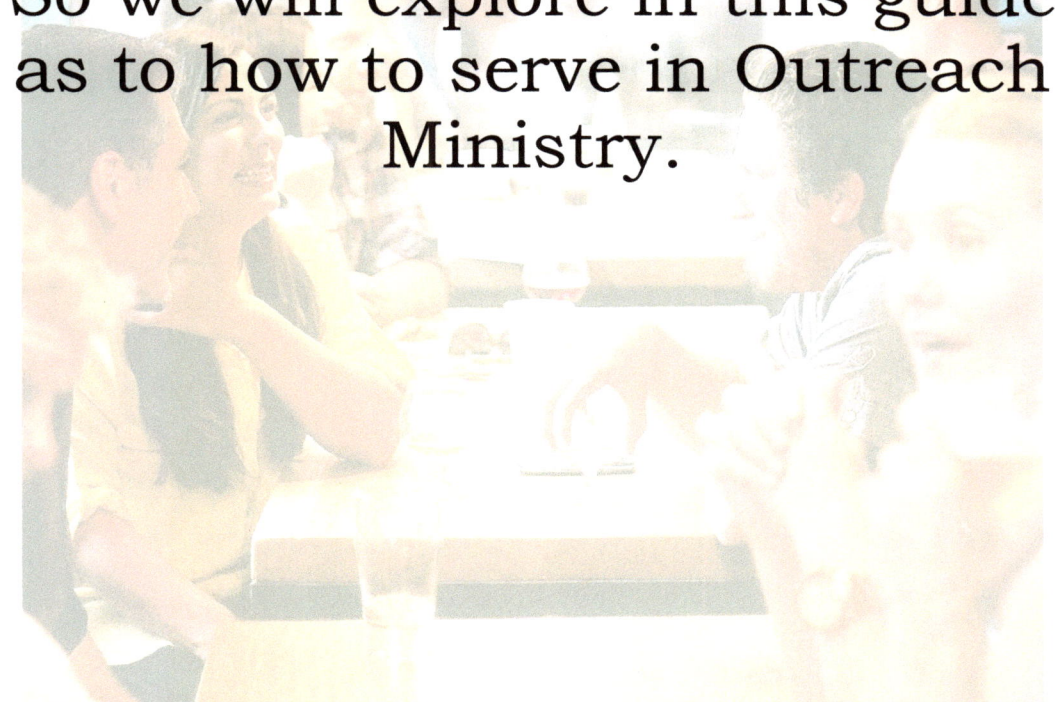

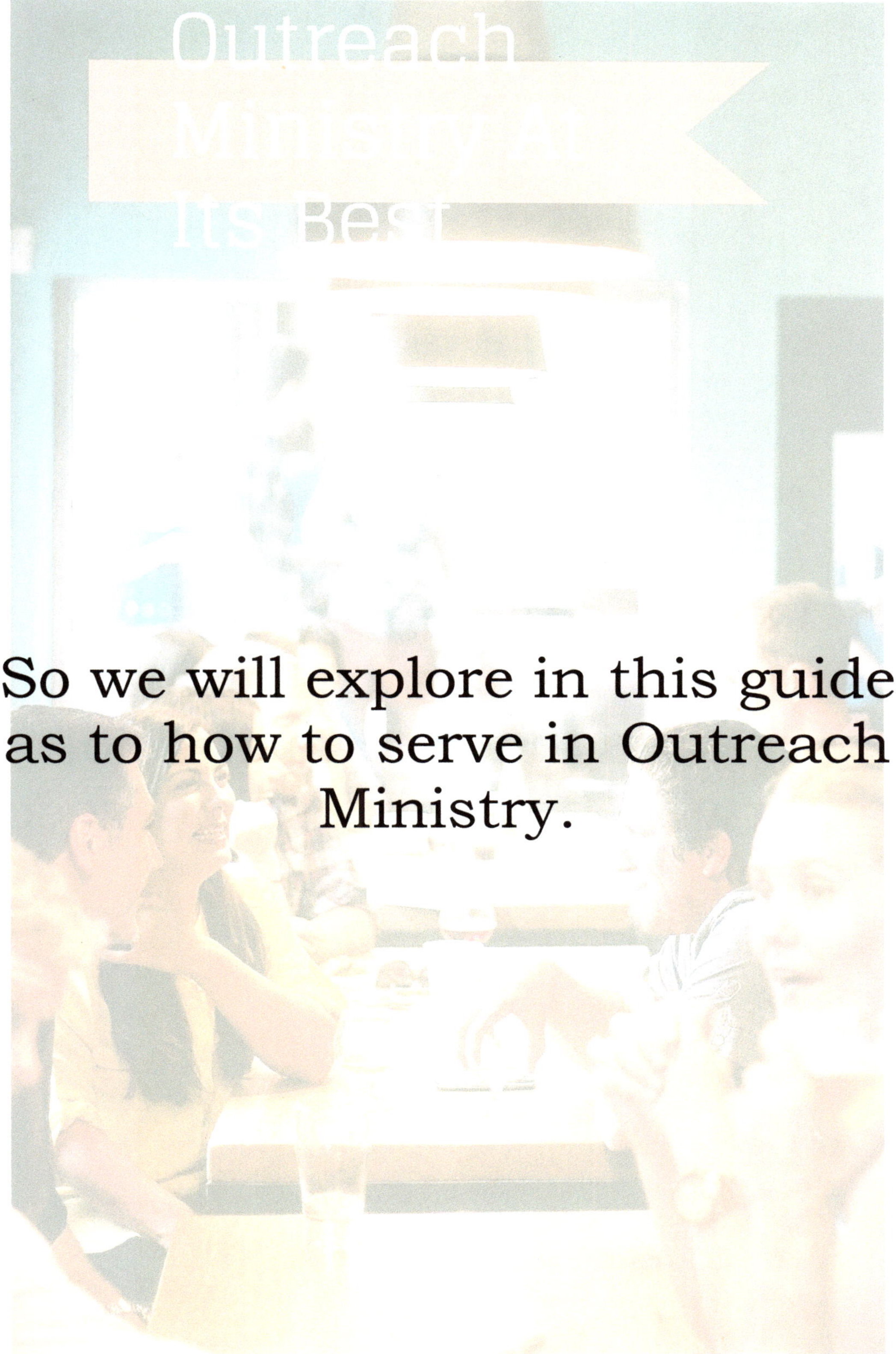

So we will explore in this guide as to how to serve in Outreach Ministry.

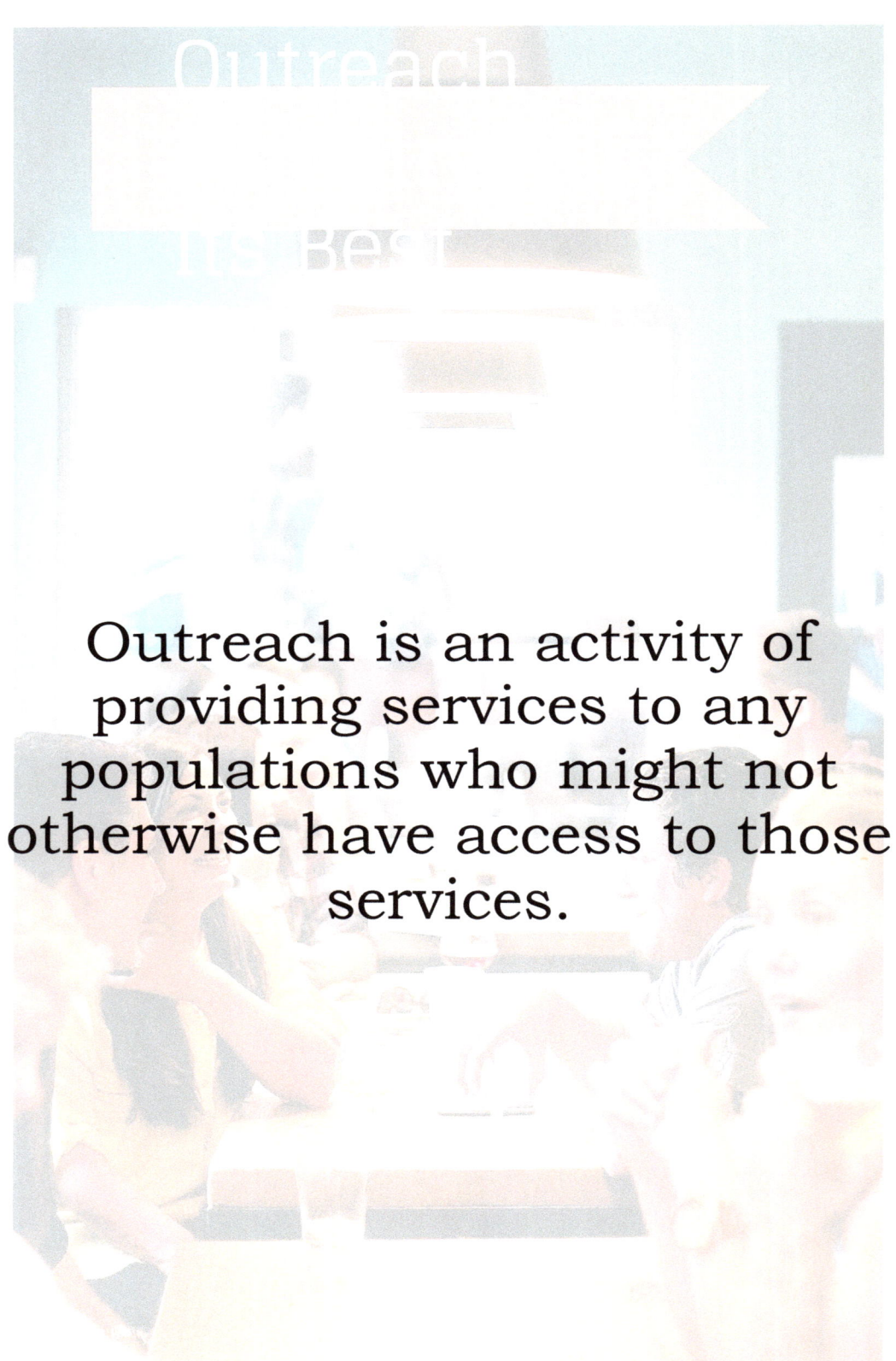

Outreach is an activity of providing services to any populations who might not otherwise have access to those services.

A key component of outreach is that the groups providing it are not stationary, but mobile; in other words, they are meeting those in need of outreach services at the locations where those in need are.

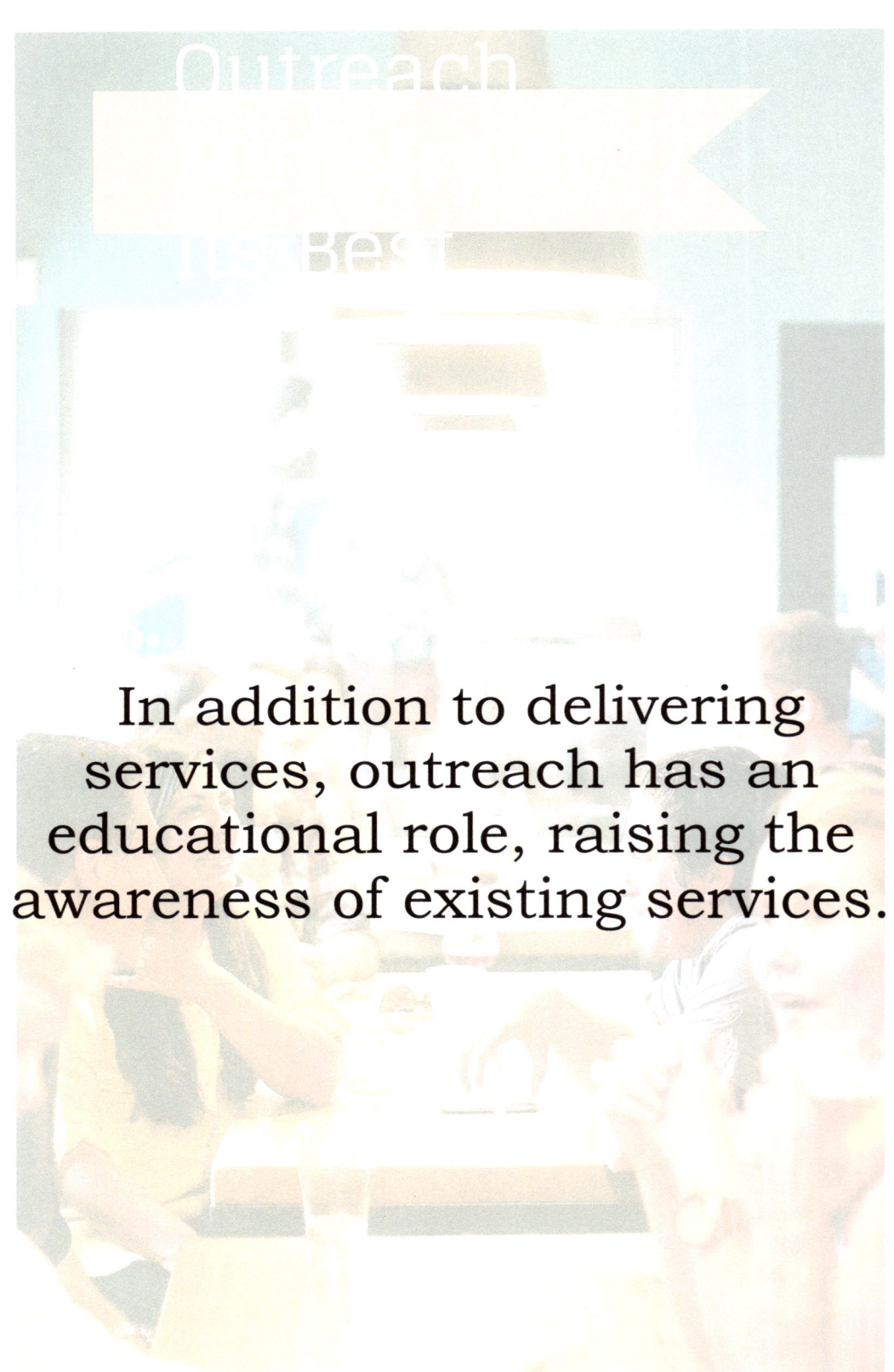

In addition to delivering services, outreach has an educational role, raising the awareness of existing services.

Outreach

Ministry At

Its Best

Outreach is often meant to fill in the gap in the services provided by mainstream (often, governmental) services, and is often carried out by non-profit, nongovernmental organizations.

This is a major element differentiating outreach from public relations. Compared to staff providing traditional services.

Outreach Ministry also refers to the gifts of help. There are those whom have a hear to help others. They will be found in Outreach Ministries.

How can we become more effective in this distinct task? Here are some ways to help your next Outreach event.

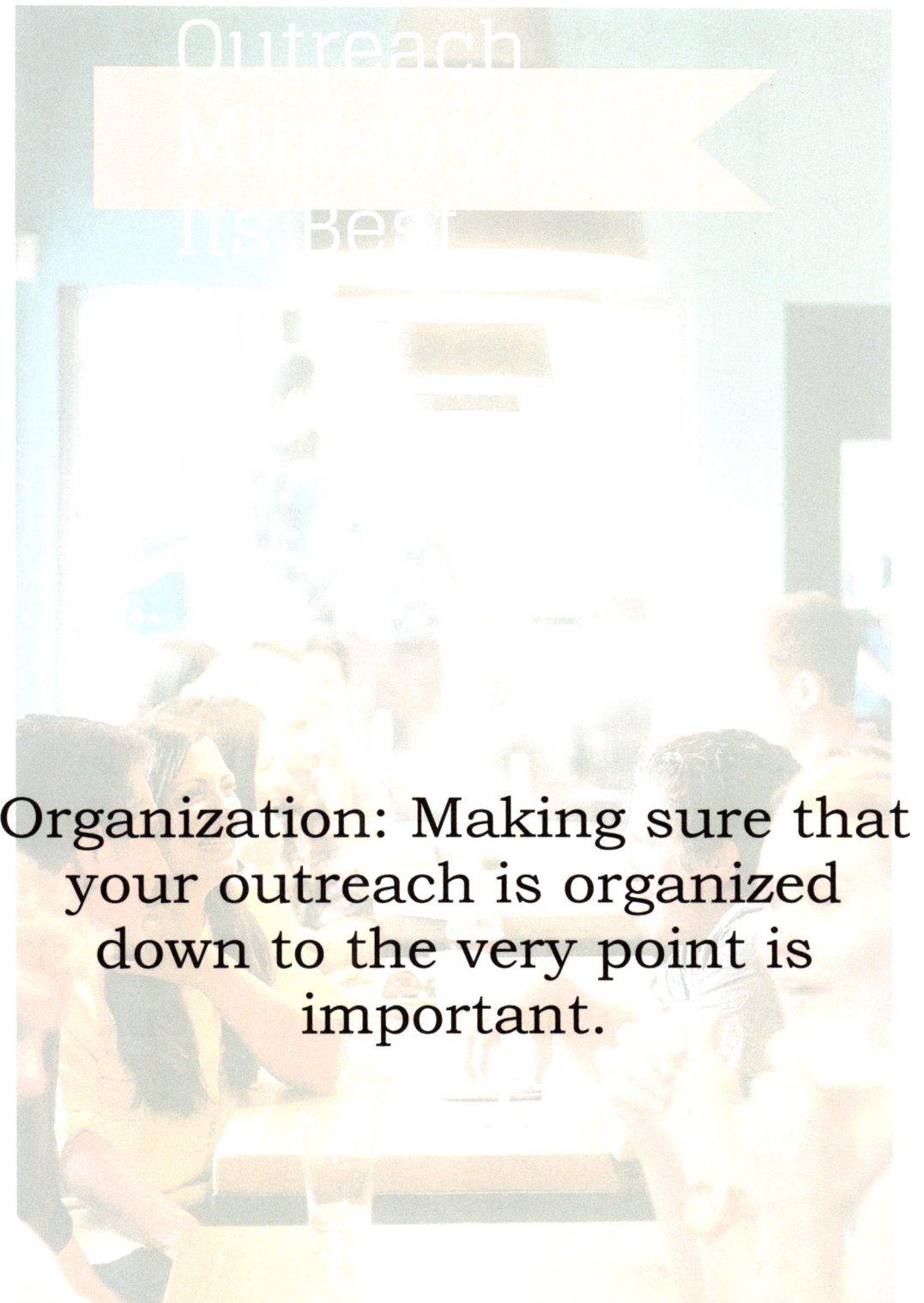

Organization: Making sure that your outreach is organized down to the very point is important.

You must take the opportunity to plan. You may not get everything right on the first and second event; but strategic planning will help you to learn by organizing your event properly.

What do you need to plan? You will need to plan the when, what, where, who, and how. time, place, people, refreshments, signs, revenue, and leadership.

As the leader, you will need more leaders. You cannot pull-off an event alone; you will need help and support. Selecting other team captains(leaders) will help assist you in this.

Building a good team is essential for success. You should select those whom have a desire to help others. If you appoint someone to perform the task; then they will be less attentive and effective.

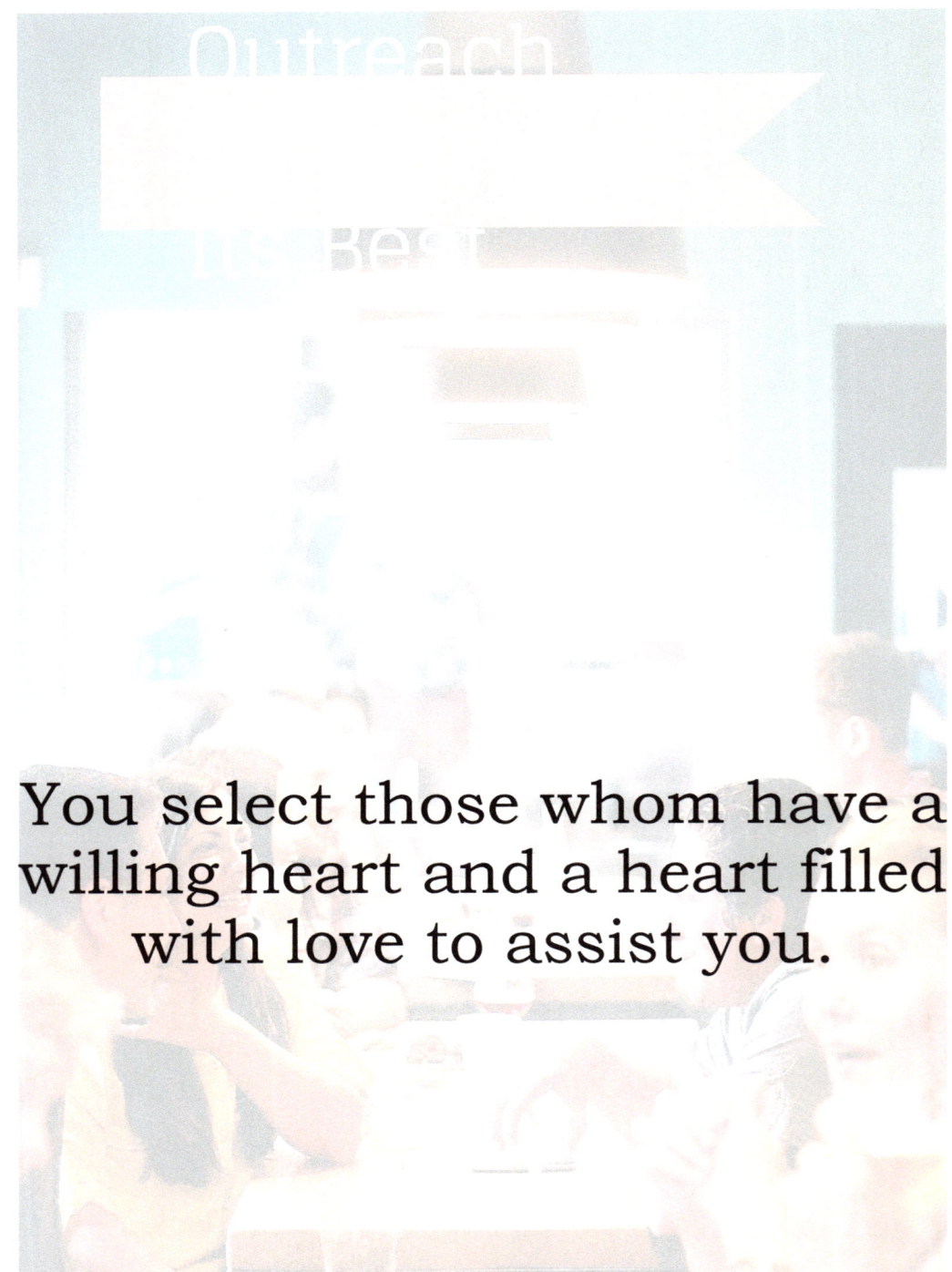

You select those whom have a willing heart and a heart filled with love to assist you.

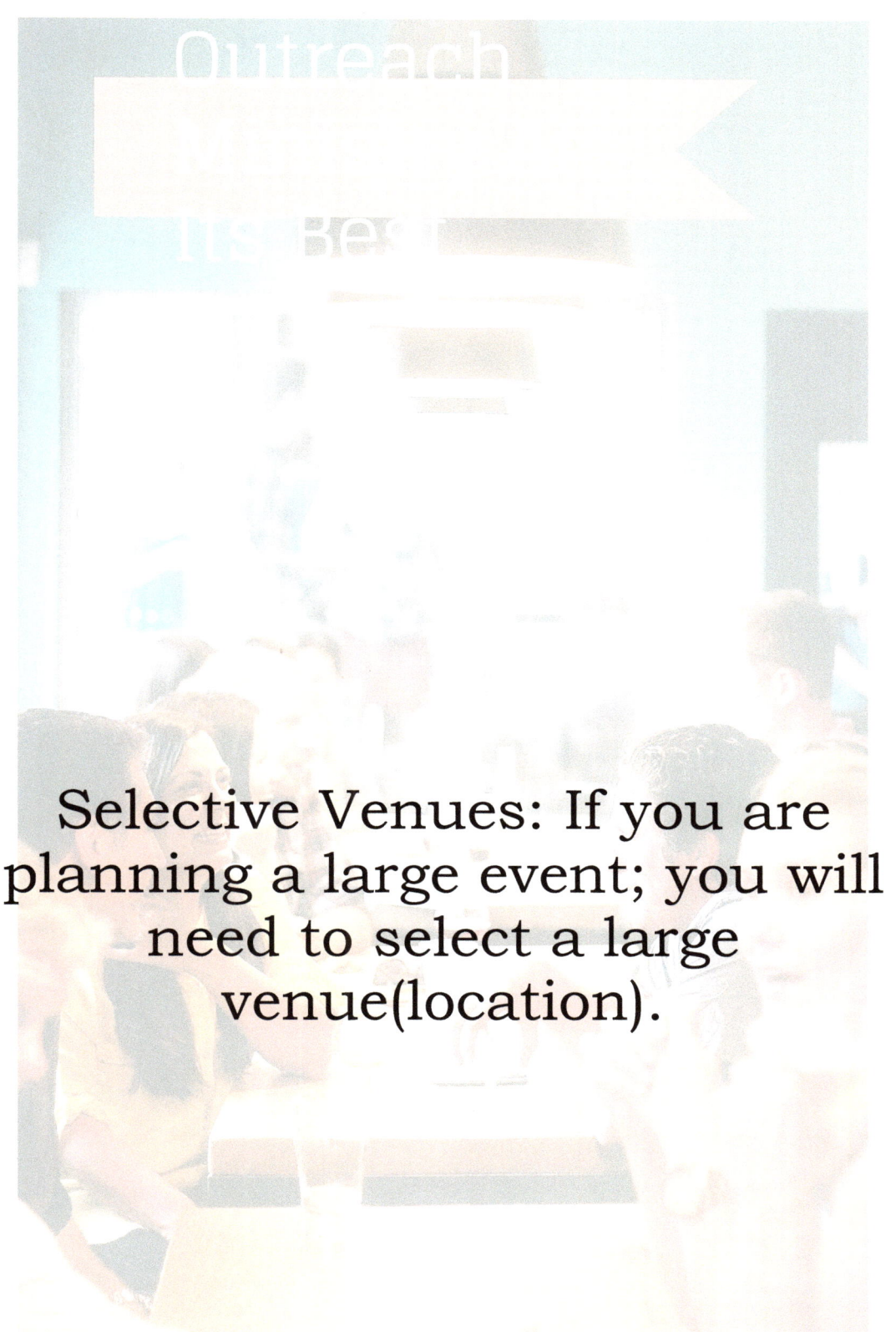

Selective Venues: If you are planning a large event; you will need to select a large venue(location).

Once you and your team leaders have selected your venue; ask the staff when you could stop by to look at the venue.

Make sure that your attire is professional but comfortable. Because you will perhaps be walking or talking a lot while screening the venue.

Bring your checklist to the venue. The checklist could consist of things as cleanliness of the bathroom and area, parking lot, other rooms at the venue, and more.

You never select a venue without conducting a walk-through of the place. This will allow you to have a full description of how your tables and chairs and products will look in the area.

It would be sad or critical if you show up for an event and you have more tables and chairs than the size of the room. Most venues will have a diagram which details the position of the tables and chairs for setup.

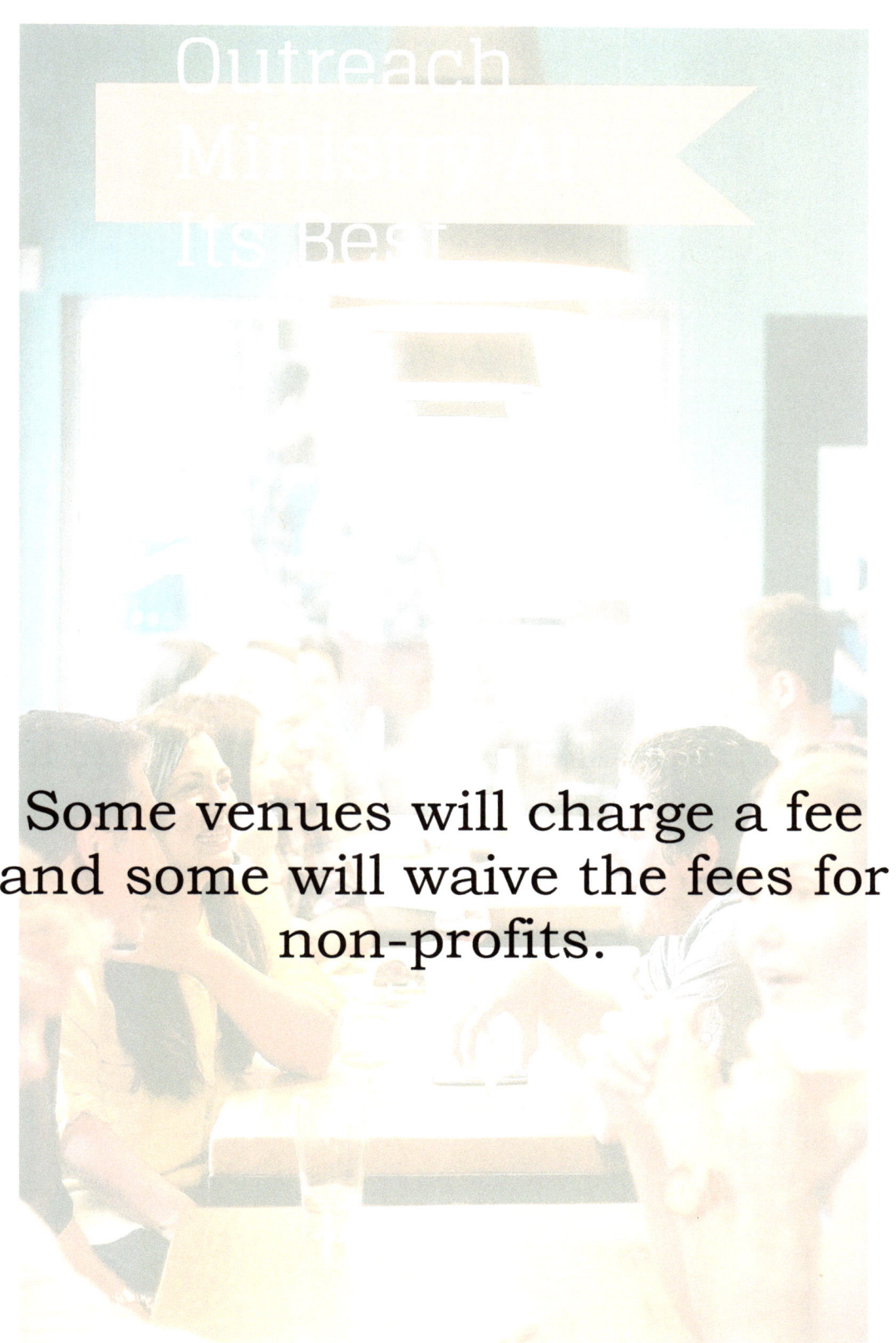

Some venues will charge a fee and some will waive the fees for non-profits.

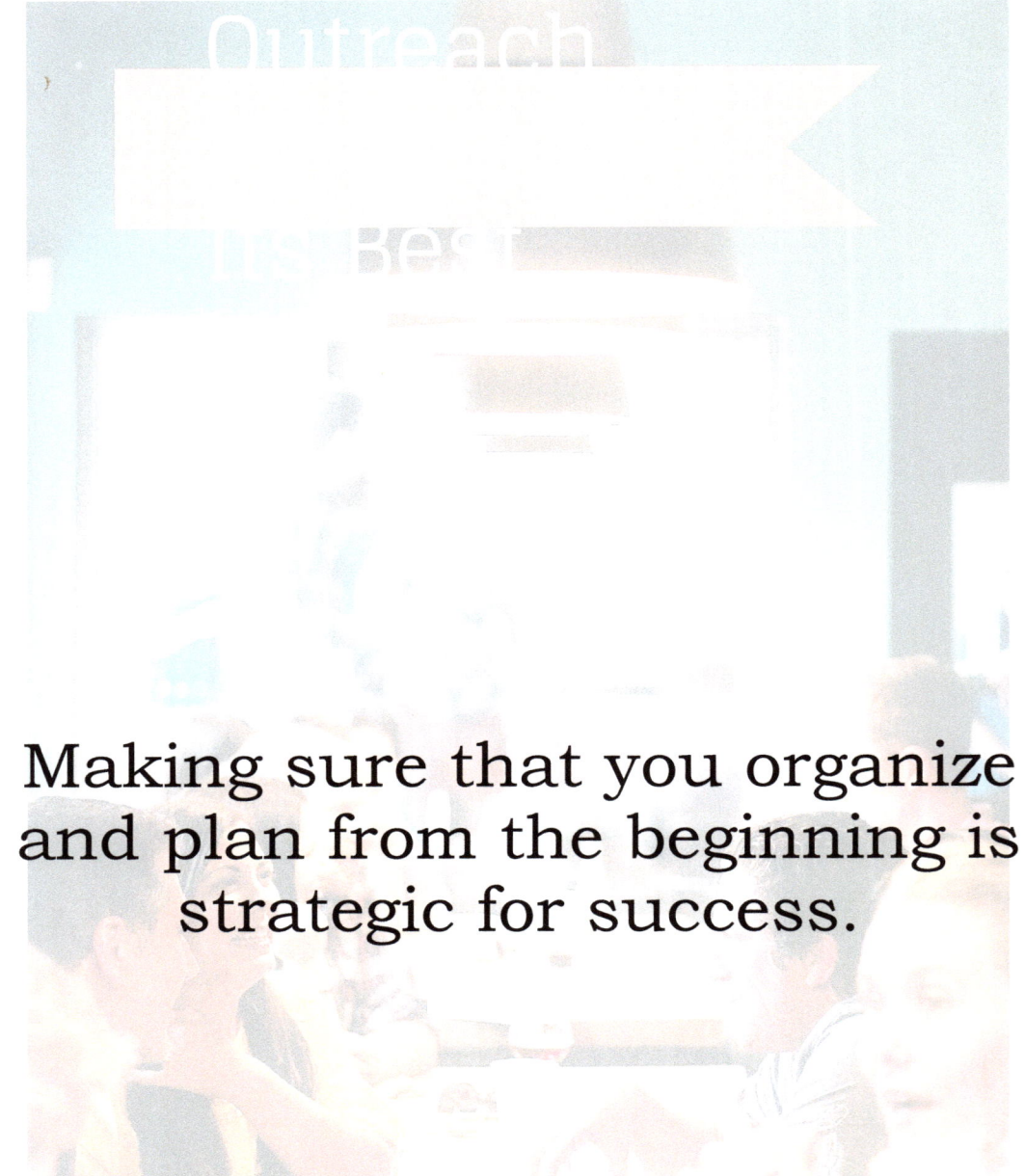

Making sure that you organize and plan from the beginning is strategic for success.

Checking the restrooms for cleanliness, outside parking lot for excessive debris, what other organization will be in the building while you are there is important.

Too many organizations in one building can create a bottle-neck. Your attendants or guests will become confused as to where to go for service.

Check with your local Chamber of Commerce for upcoming events. You want your event to have a great attendance and turn out.

For example: If you are planning an event to give away food and clothes; and there is a *"Relay for Life"* event scheduled in your local area; then your crowd will be at The *"Relay for Life" event.* People tend to follow the crowd.

Follow up with your team captains to make sure that everything is ready-to-go days before the event.

Follow up with the director of the venue to see if there is additional equipment which you will need; such as podiums, audio, more chairs, bull-horn(s), etc.

If you have missed something; this is okay. There isn't anything wrong about missing something. Find out what it is and correct the problem.

Make sure that your team leaders are staffed with volunteers. These will be your runners. Your runners should be performing just that. They shouldn't be all over the place; only in the positions where they are needed.

For example: If Terry is positioned to issue bottled water; this is what Terry should be doing. Consult with your team leaders that they shouldn't pull volunteers from others team leaders' groups. Once people began to get out of place; it will be difficult to control their movement.

There are many team leaders; but only one Captain Leader. Remember the old saying; "Too many chiefs, but not enough Indians." This can be controlled once the Organizer/Host is aware of what he or she should be leading this outreach.

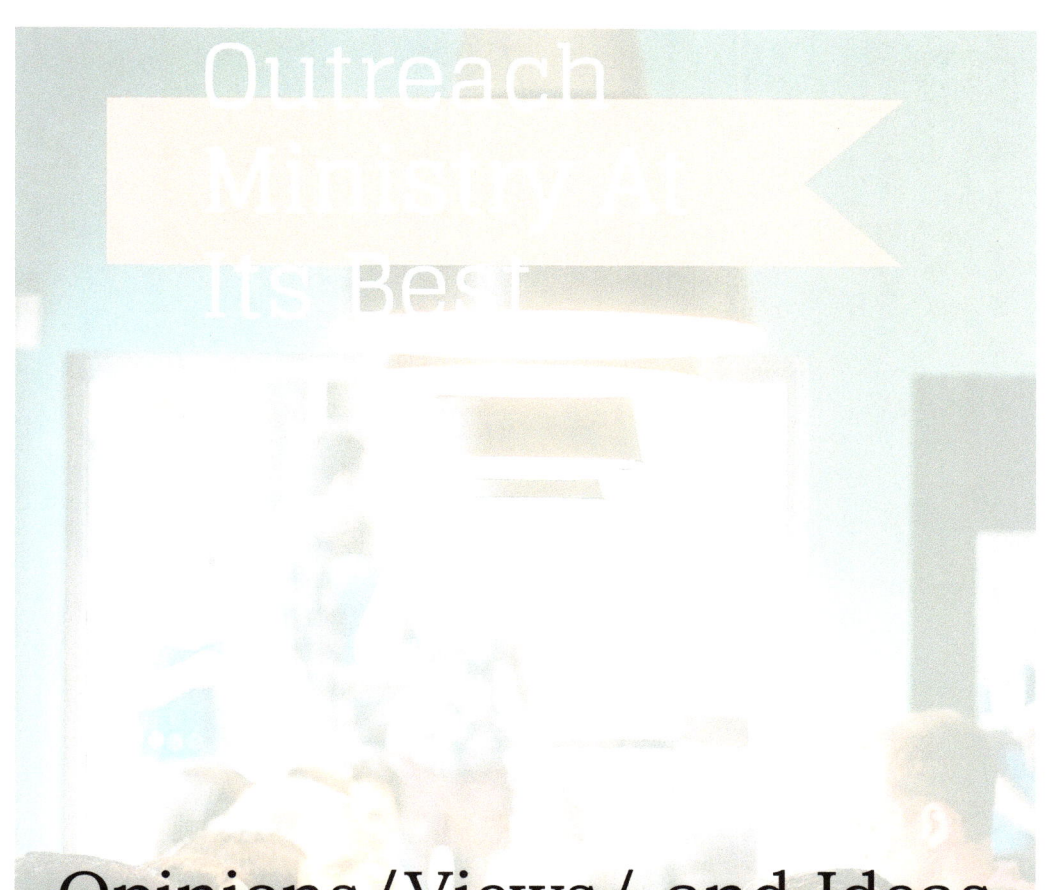

Opinions/Views/ and Ideas should be welcomed from your team leaders; but the organizer/host should be the last word for the event.

Set a goal/mission/ and or vision for your event. This will allow your volunteers/participants/attendants/ and or team leaders to get a full panoramic view of your purpose.

The participants/attendants will grasp the emotional effect of your purpose for having the event. Why is this important? As I stated; you want your participants to see your cause. Many organizations host outreach events in order to gain publicity.

Outreach

is Best

Outreach Ministry should never be hosted to gain repetition/reputation/ or publicity. This should be a heart-felt, heart-motivated effort.

Your participants will feel your passion to help and assist others. Now; you can invite the media out to cover your event. There is nothing wrong with that.

But make sure that your motives are aligned correctly. Because others will know if your intentions are pure.

Be courteous to your participants. They showed an effort to support you, so return that support by being kind and not having a bad day in their presence.

Sponsors: This will help you in a huge financial way or ways for incentives. There are businesses which are waiting to get recognized through your event.

Get one of your team leaders to type out a "Letter-head-proposal for several local businesses in your area. You don't need to reach out to national businesses/charities for your local event.

Allow those around you to spotlight their business/organization/church. Sponsors also help your event to reach more people.

Make sure that you contact/notify your potential sponsors in an ample time frame so that they can order additional incentives for your participants. Thank them before and after your event.

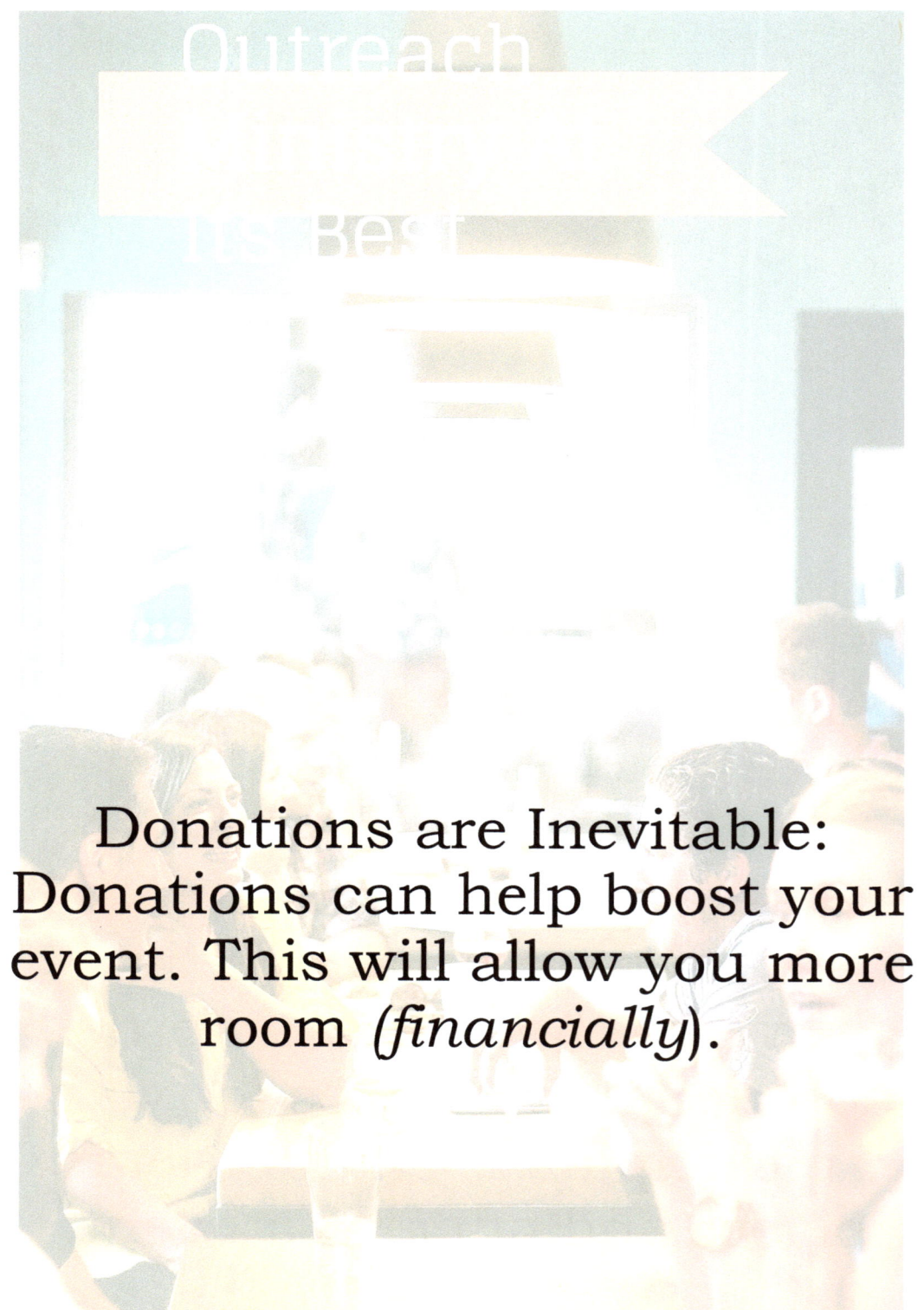

Donations are Inevitable: Donations can help boost your event. This will allow you more room *(financially)*.

Free Advertising: Your local television broadcast, newspaper, social media, radio broadcast, featured articles, are all great ways to spread the word. All of these platforms are free of charge.

Count up the Cost: Count the cost of your event. This will include refreshments if being served; venue if you are being charged; city permits for event; etc.

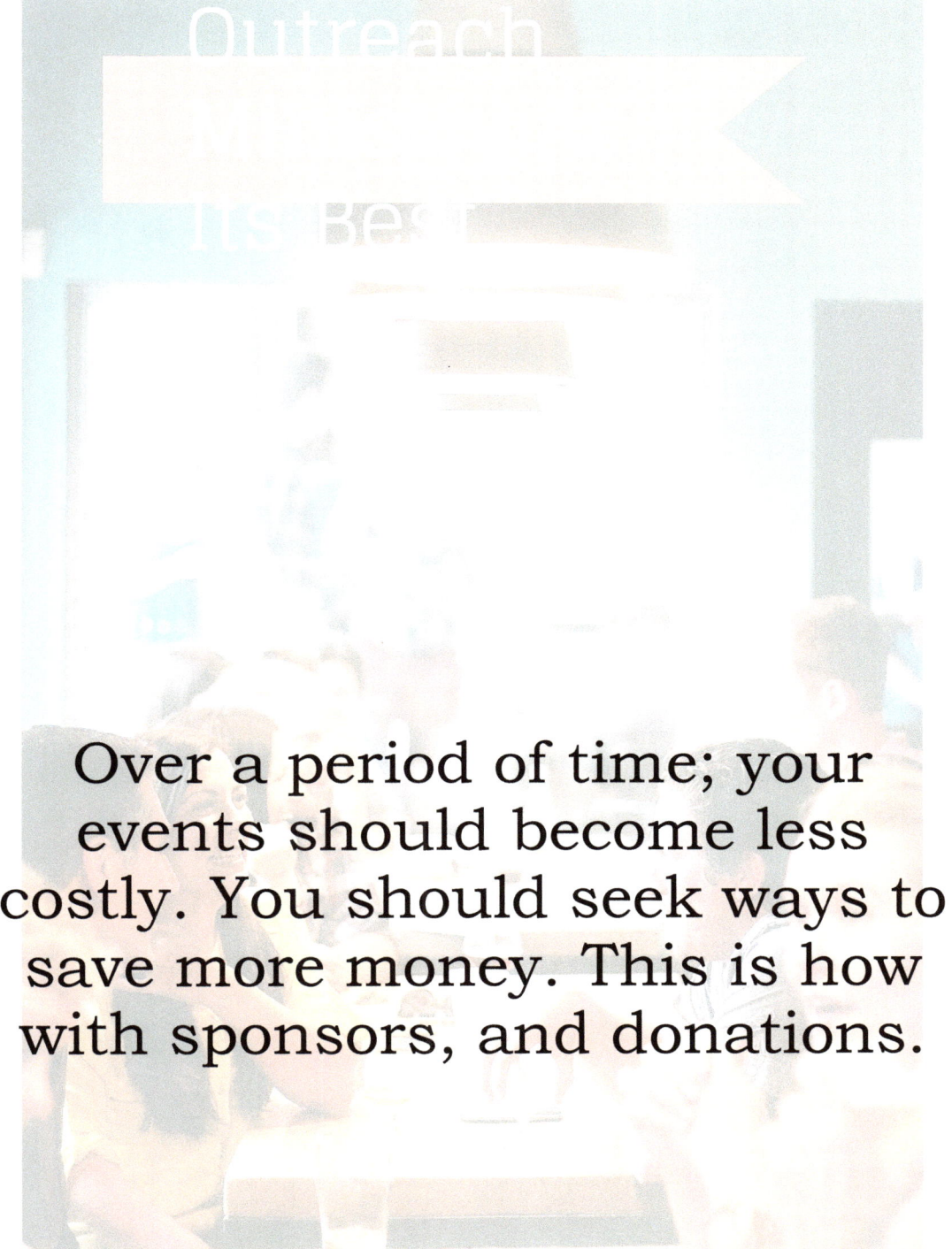

Over a period of time; your events should become less costly. You should seek ways to save more money. This is how with sponsors, and donations.

Giving to Local Charities: If you've organized an outreach event; seek ways to give a portion back to a local charity; or the remaining items to your local charity.

Remember the scriptures from Luke 6; "Give and it shall be given you; press down, shaken together, running over, that men will give unto your bosom.

Time: Planning a time for start to end is essential. After two hours; you can lose peoples' interest of your event. It doesn't take a long time to complete a wonderful thing.

If you have a food pantry ministry with your local food bank; remain focus and true to your agreement. Many churches get focused upon trying to win souls to Christ with food or clothing.

This is the in correct approach for outreach ministry. If your intentions and motives are true and wholesome; they will see the Christ within you. Most food banks will allow up to 20 minutes to interact with the participant.

Stick to your vision/mission of why you are hosting the event and they will return. We should serve without holding participants under any obligations. They are free to choose if they desire to pray, listen to a brief sermon, etc.

This shouldn't be an option for them to participate neither inquired of the participant. Just plan the event as it should be so that you don't tire out the participants nor your volunteers. They may have something else to do for the day.

They shouldn't have to sift and filter through obligation which you desire for them to have. Give and let them leave. This also will help the volunteers to time their departure which includes clean up and arranging the venue area as they received it.

Documentation: With volunteers; create a small application for them to submit which can include name, address, phone number, emergency contact, why they desire to volunteer, physician, and any allergies.

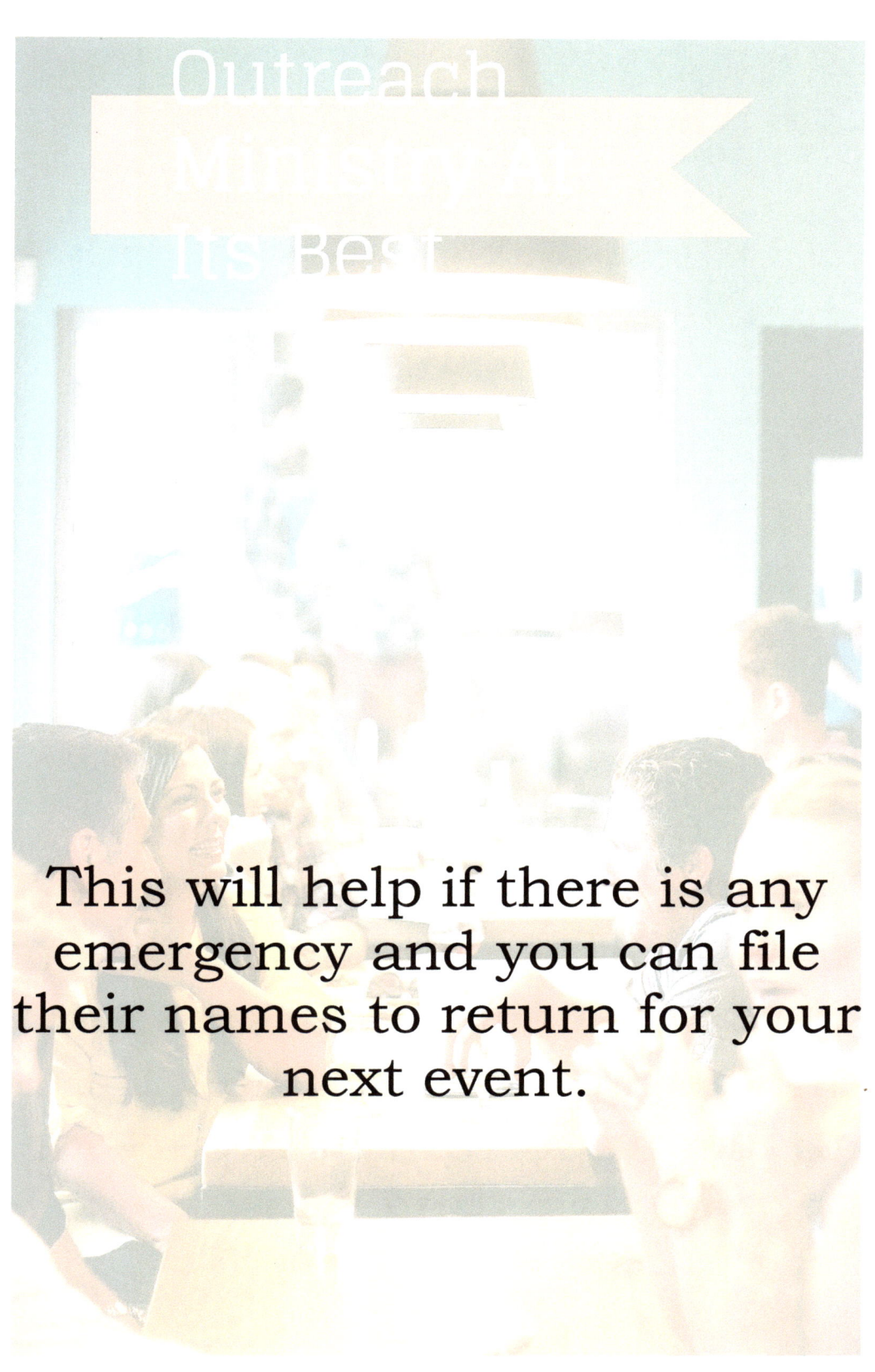

This will help if there is any emergency and you can file their names to return for your next event.

Rewards: reward your volunteers with a small token of love. This will compel them to return. Hard workers are difficult to find. So allow them to feel important or a part for assisting you.

Monitors: Make sure to have monitors to scan the area, the parking lot, the restrooms, and other areas in the venue for safety and to minimize theft or criminal activity.

Although our intentions are good; but we must always plan for the "What-Ifs." Anything can occur and we must be ready and prepared.

With these minimal tools and resources; your outreach ministry should and will be a great success. With having the opportunity to plan over 157 events within the last 3 years; I am sure that your next outreach will be a success.